Pushkin Press —

It was not easy to be a sportswoman at the end of the nineteenth century. Pierre de Coubertin, founder of the modern Olympic Games, said in 1896: "No matter how toughened a sportswoman may be, her organism is not cut out to sustain certain shocks." Women competed in the Olympics for the first time in 1900.

The "white sailor hats" and the "confusion between you, your hat, and the ball" in Lady Greville's book may now seem charmingly old-fashioned—until we remember that in 2015, more than a century later, more than 40% of elite sportswomen in Britain were reported to have suffered sexism. Which suddenly makes the bold gentlewomen of 1892 seem far more pioneering...

The books in "Found on the Shelves" have been chosen to give a fascinating insight into the treasures that can be found while browsing in The London Library. Now celebrating its 175th anniversary, with over seventeen miles of shelving and more than a million books, The London Library has become an unrivalled archive of the modes, manners and thoughts of each generation which has helped to form it.

From essays on dieting in the 1860s to instructions for gentlewomen on trout-fishing, from advice on the ill health caused by the "modern" craze of bicycling to travelogues from Norway, they are as readable and relevant today as they were more than a century ago— even if contemporary sportswomen no longer have to "thank Providence and one's tailor for one's knickerbockers"!

THE GENTLEWOMAN'S BOOK OF SPORTS

The London Library

Pushkin Press

Pushkin Press
71–75 Shelton Street
London WC2H 9JQ

Selection and editorial material © Pushkin Press and The London
Library 2016

Chapters selected from *The Gentlewoman's Book of Sports, 1*, edited
by Lady Greville (The Victoria Library for Gentlewomen), London:
Henry & Co., 1892

Illustrations from C.J. Longman and Col. H. Walrond, *Archery*. London:
Longmans, Green and Co., 1894

First published by Pushkin Press in 2016

9 8 7 6 5 4 3 2 1

ISBN 978 1 782272 47 2

All rights reserved. No part of this publication may be reproduced,
stored in a retrieval system or transmitted in any form or by any means,
electronic, mechanical, photocopying, recording or otherwise, without
prior permission in writing from Pushkin Press

Set in Goudy Modern by Tetragon, London

Printed by CPI Group (UK) Ltd, Croydon, CR0 4YY

www.pushkinpress.com

THE GENTLEWOMAN'S BOOK OF SPORTS

EDITED BY
LADY GREVILLE, 1892

LADY VIOLET GREVILLE (1842–1932) was an author by profession who became, in the 1880s and 1890s, the writer of a ladies column in the *Graphic*. She joined The London Library on 19th October 1897, giving her occupation as "Lady".

Preface

A keen love of sport is inherent in the breast of all true Englishmen; and the desire of adventure, the disregard of comfort and danger, that it encourages, have gone far to make them the conquerors of the world. In times, like the present, of morbid self-analysis and diseased introspection, a return to nature, to wholesome healthy amusement and field sports, cannot be too strongly encouraged. The sportsman is not cruel, as has sometimes been wantonly asserted: he loves animals, birds, insects, flowers and all the beauties of nature. In his lonely wanderings face to face with the glorious aspect of sea and sky, of the bleak mountain side and the luxuriant valley, he studies the habits of wild beasts, the ways of feathered fowl, the lore and knowledge of herbs and plants. He learns to love the country for its own sake; to appreciate its poetry, its glamour, its healthful peace; to admire and enjoy "the broken sunlight glinting through copse and gleaming on fern, the woodland sights, the woodland sounds, the balmy odours of Nature, and all the treats she provides for her votaries."

In like manner, many women have cultivated habits of endurance, of observation, of activity, of courage and self-command, of patience and energy. The record of some of their adventures and pastimes will, I venture to think, be favourably received by the public, and may encourage other women, as feminine but more timid, to imitate their achievements, and to acquire a keen zest for and sympathy with outdoor pursuits.

Each of the ladies who contribute to this volume may claim to be an authority——so far as her own sex is concerned——on the subject of which she treats; and it is thought that these reminiscences and suggestions may be of service to other ladies who are merely beginning to interest themselves in the sports discoursed upon.

VIOLET GREVILLE

TROUT-FISHING

BY LADY COLIN CAMPBELL

LADY COLIN CAMPBELL (née Gertrude Elizabeth Blood) was best known for the divorce scandal which shocked Victorian society. After four years of marriage, she sued for divorce on grounds of her husband's infidelity and cruelty. Lord Colin alleged that his wife had committed adultery with at least four men. No divorce was obtained, and she became a successful writer and editor (see "Fencing").

In the majority of sports and athletics, the question of the surroundings amongst which they are pursued is an all-important one; and, perhaps, in none is the question more obstinately to the fore than in Trout-fishing. The inexhaustible charm of that delightful sport does not by any means solely depend on the number or size of the speckled beauties one returns home with, fagged, wet, but triumphant, after a long day's fishing. To catch a 60-lb. salmon in the Serpentine would not be worth crossing Hyde Park for; and it is the surroundings of moorland or copse, babbling brown mountain stream, or purling lowland brook, as well as the knowledge that only art and patience will enable you to get the better of your wily prey, which give you that sense of intense satisfaction and triumph with which you wend your way homewards, proudly conscious of the weight of the well-filled basket that is the best testimony to your knowledge of this so-called "gentle art."

No one who is a blood-thirsty hunter, as the average Englishman is popularly and incorrectly supposed to be, would care much for a sport which he would probably designate contemptuously as "mild"; but, after all, any given moment can only hold a certain measure of excitement, and to the true trout-fisher it is an open question whether that measure is not as surely reached when she pulls a monster that weighs three-quarters of a pound out of a mountain stream with the aid of a tiny American 8-oz. rod, a hair-gut line, and a fly little bigger than the familiar midge, as in that supreme moment in a Terai jungle, when a tiger rushes out from his lair amongst the waving canes under the very nose of the sportsman's elephant. Size in sport is only relative, and success and surroundings are everything.

To the artistic sense the surroundings of trout-fishing——the river, large or small, with its bubbling eddies, its broken boulders, rocky bed, and stony runs, the trembling shadows of the black poplars or alders, the wide stretches of moorland as one climbs to the upper waters of the stream——offer an endless attraction; while the artistic features of the sport itself, the delicacy of hand, the unerring aim and quickness of eye, the necessity of knowing how to take advantage of every passing cloud, of every corner or boulder of rock, keep the faculties of the sportswoman for ever on the alert, banishing all consciousness of fatigue or wet garments. Who is there that has ever fished a river, whether it be the broad and majestic Tay or Namsen, or a little mountain stream one could almost jump across, with that ever-present and persistent hope of catching a bigger leviathan than was ever caught before, that will not admit with me that trout-fishing has an inexhaustible charm that even the slaying of the mighty salmon does not quench the enjoyment of? Innumerable, too, are the ways whereby we may attempt to beguile our prey in trout-fishing. The salmon is often a sulky beast; he may have been long in the river, have lost his bright, silvery scales, and become a red, torpid monster; the water may not be of the approved height which will prompt his peculiar taste for taking notice of your fly or bait; the wind may be in the wrong direction, or the perpetual "Heaven knows why!" may be the only possible explanation of his irritating contumacy; but it often happens that you may fish patiently all day, expending a zeal which you end by thinking worthy of a better cause, flaunting the most tempting flies the mind of Farlow can conceive and create, watching the salmon jumping perpetually all around you, and yet not getting a vestige of sport from a single fish. Not so with the game little trout. Tell me of a mountain stream of clear brown water, deep black pools, and rocky bed, that has not been visited that spring by that person of one's detestation, a brother sportsman who fishes one's favourite pools before one gets a chance of doing so; let it be a nice mild day with a cloudy sky, and a slight tendency to drizzle, "a wee bit saft," as they say in Scotland; give me my fishing-basket, landing-net, small 8-oz. rod of split cane, and a little pocket-book of different coloured midges; and dressed in a pair of tweed knickerbockers, kilt skirt, loose, many-pocketed coat, woollen stockings, and thick, hob-nailed shoes, out of which the water can "squelch" as easily as it enters, I will begin my fishing with a delightful certainty of not returning home *bredouillée* after my day's sport is over.

I begin at as low a point down stream as is convenient, and otter-wise I proceed to wade up-stream, fishing pool after pool right up into the lonely moorland above (from whose peat the stream derives its lovely clear brown colour, as well as the animalculae that trout love to eat so greedily), until the burn becomes so narrow that you would hardly think a trout could turn round in it. At one moment I am standing at the lower end of a pool with the water coming bubbling down a little cascade in front of me. The pool above me I can hardly see, yet I know that by an intelligent cast with a long line over my left shoulder I shall avoid an ugly black poplar-tree on my right, which the wind, that is blowing in my face, might well hang my line up in; and I drop my fly, some twenty or thirty feet ahead, behind a big boulder where the water is boiling. It is a hundred to one that I shall get a trout there. The trout are taking a little short; I drop my fly with the greatest caution in the spot required. The little monster of the pool rushes promptly to the surface; but I have withdrawn my fly with such rapidity, and with such care not to splash the water, that the trout leaps angrily into the air after the bait that has vanished. This is a form of strategy that holds good in many encounters in life; and having thus raised his expectations and baulked him in his first attempt (which was probably only intended to drown the fly, not to take it), in my next cast I leave the line upon the water. He dashes furiously at it, and the next instant he flies across the pool, making the little rod bend as if he were a 60-lb. salmon; but the struggle does not last long, and he is presently transferred to my basket.

A little further on, my progress up-stream is apparently stopped by another cascade between two high walls of rock that enclose the little river in a gorge; but obstacles of this kind should never stop a trout-fisher. Clambering over boulders, and jumping from stone to stone, I gain the bank. Once there, I see I can scramble through some bushes and fir trees, and over a heathery knoll whence I can look down on the secluded little pool below into which the little waterfall is falling with ceaseless bubble and song. I *know* the trout must be lying either right under the little white tongue of spray, or else further down the pool where the water begins to thin out and the stones can just be seen at the bottom. I try the former place as being the more likely. Two trout rise at the same time, and both are hooked. Now begin the difficulties of the situation. The trout, beautiful monsters of half a pound each, are rushing wildly around the pool. I am thirty feet above them. What can I do? I cannot get at them with the landing-net, and I certainly cannot haul them up with my little rod and my hair-gut line. I survey the surroundings, and almost decide to lower myself past an alder-bush on to a rock, when I fortunately perceive another bush below again which would infallibly catch my line; so I give that up, and turn my attention to the possibilities of a little ledge below me. If I can reach it, I can from thence get right down to the stone over which the little cataract is pouring; and by getting my trout into the side eddy, and by tiring them out completely, I may succeed, with great care, in reaching them one by one.

To read about such a descent is easy; but to accomplish it with one hand occupied in holding a rod to which are attached, only by a hair-gut line, two turbulent trout, is a very different matter; and the difficulties of the precipitous descent cause one to thank Providence and one's tailor for one's knicker-bockers. However, I have all but reached the place, and am almost ready for the final struggle with my prey, who, in the meantime, are tugging at one another to the imminent peril of the cast, when a treacherously slippery stone betrays me, and I come to unholy grief in the upper pool, with my knee hard against a rock, half way up to my waist in water, and a bitter consciousness filling my soul that my lunch, which is located in my pocket, is probably reduced to wet pap by that unlucky slip. But all these are minor ills, that are forgotten in the glorious fact that the trout are still there on my line in the pool below. I wind up the line carefully, take my landing-net off my back, and making the best use of my immersed position, I spoon out the first one; and, as luck will have it, the second is so exhausted I secure him too. I wade to the bank, and sitting down among the bilberries and moss take out and examine, with triumphant joy, the two leviathans that have cost me so much trouble, a barked knee, and a partial wetting. The latter necessitates the preventive of a thimbleful of whisky,—without a little flask of which no wise trout-fisher will set out on a day's fishing,—and after discussing some of the soaked lunch with a ravenous appetite, I continue on my way up stream with varying success, until by the time I have reached and left the upper waters in the moorland, and am on my homeward journey, my basket is heavy enough to make me proudly conscious of its weight.

But this is not the only form of trout-fishing, though to my mind it is far the best and most enjoyable. I know mountain lakes where real leviathans of 3 and 4 lbs. each may be obtained; but this form of fishing is done from a boat. There should be a good stiff breeze blowing, and the boat should be kept some forty or fifty yards from the shore. Towards the shore I cast, using a Nottingham reel and a minnow (a deadly bait), letting the minnow run out the reel, not with the ability, no doubt, of a true Nottingham lad,——but then you have to begin as a baby in long clothes to achieve this art, and avoid the reel over-winding and putting your line in a tangle so complete that five minutes, and language "more true than tellable," have to be got through before the line allows itself to be straightened once more. But with ordinary care these tangles may be avoided, and many a monster may be caught in this fashion. In many lakes the trout will not look at a small fly, just as in many rivers they will not look at a minnow. In the Norwegian lakes four- or five-pounders are often caught with a minnow and a Nottingham reel; but unfortunately the intelligent, or rather the unintelligent, Norse natives have been taught to poach with an "otter," composed of large flies, which they trail round the shore line or over the beds where the trout lie, and for the hundreds they catch for salting for winter food they frighten and wound many more, which are always lost from struggling on the line of an "otter." When one of these lakes has been unpoached, as when a stream has been unfished for a year or two, one is certain to have a magnificent day's sport if the weather is in the least favourable.

Everything, however, is artificially made nowadays, and in the same way that the inhabitants of country villas make sham rockwork to ornament their suburban gardens, so the art of trout breeding has been practised in hundreds of localities with very considerable success. Almost any stream (provided you clear out the chub and jack), even a sedgy, sluggish ditch, such as flows through many of our low country meadows, could be made into what the London cockney would think a magnificent trout river. You can fill it to repletion with big, fat trout, which you can pull out with a rod and fly, much as the monks of old used to pull out the carp and tench with nets from their fishponds. You have only to arrange a little breeding-place, strip your trout in the spawning season, hatch the fry in little gravel pans of running water, and educate them in a succession of reservoirs, where you feed and stuff them with ground liver, and in a year's time you can turn out into your "trout stream" pretty nearly as many fish as you choose. But do not complain if the trout, bred and fed in this artificial way, is as different a creature to the wild, game little speckled beauty of a Scottish Highland stream, as a prize-fed bullock is to the black bull of an Andalusian *ganadería*.

Another form of trout-fishing I have seen less of, but which requires consummate art, is the dry-fly fishing of the Hampshire rivers. To drop a gossamer line with a May-fly inserted on a hook, without splash or ripple, or injuring the bait on the clear surface of a river among weeds and sedge is no easy task; but many is the good day's sport such rivers afford, where the trout also run to a considerable size. The perfection of trout-fishing, however, is the mountain stream. The endless variety of pool and waterfall, the pleasure and independence of being able to wade right into the water, make an entirely different sport of it, to fishing from a boat, or from the grassy bank of a sluggish brook. Needless to say that in trout-fishing, as in every sport, the choice of implements is all-important. A strong rod, with a heavy line and a big minnow, or cast of large lake flies, gives you but poor sport in pulling out even four-pounders, as against catching a half-pound trout on the beautiful light tackle which the Americans so well understand how to make. A little single-handed split-cane rod, which never tires your hand to fish with the whole day, is infinitely preferable to the two-handed "greenheart" which the English lake-fisherman is wont to employ; and the little fine brown-gut casts, which are almost like a gossamer in the air, afford a splendid opportunity for delicacy of handling a half-pound fish. One single jerk on the rod, and your cast is in two; and the fish goes back sadder and wiser to the bottom of the pool with half a yard of cast in his mouth.

As to flies, there is absolutely no end to the fads of fishers on the subject. The salmon-fisher will sit and gloat over his fly-book of silk-bodied, pig-wool, red or orange feathered flies, in an ecstasy of contemplation. Like a French cook, ruminating over what dish he can invent to tickle the jaded palate of his master, the salmon-fisher turns over his "Jock-Scott" and "Blue Doctor," or hundreds of other combinations of wool, silk, and feathers, wondering what is most likely to tempt the salmon of the river he mostly affects. The trout, however, is not so aesthetic and fastidious in his tastes. A brownish fly or a black one, with a little bit of red, green or yellow in the hackle, invariably suits him. The mallard's wing, the grouse, and the guinea fowl afford the feathers for the best combinations. Unlike the salmon, he never aspires to the golden pheasant's suit of splendid gold; a little tuft of yellow wool in the tail of the fly satisfies the modest tastes of the trout. The consequence is that trout-flies are a very cheap commodity, and a very few shillings will purchase all the flies you could either flick away or fish away on a trout-fishing excursion. In the matter of reels, the small light reels that are now made are quite delightful, as they will exactly balance a little split-cane rod. Nothing is so important as this: a rod, whether for salmon or trout, should *balance*, as a gun should, perfectly. The hand, when grasping the rod in its proper position, should feel the weight just evenly distributed, neither top-heavy nor butt-heavy as the case may be; otherwise it will seriously interfere with your casting, and spoil the delicacy of your hand. Some fishermen get into a very rough method of flogging their line down on the water and making a heavy trail, which, though it does not signify in salmon-fishing, where the fly has always to float down-stream before it works up-stream over the salmon, is a very great disadvantage in trout-fishing. Trout, like all fish, lie with their heads up-stream, but the trout has a totally different way of taking a fly to that of a salmon. For a trout it is always best to throw the fly *up-stream*, and drop it over his nose, hence the lighter the line falls upon the water altogether, the less likely he will be to be disturbed.

The salmon, on the other hand, in many cases follows the fly across the stream, or rises at it as it sweeps by him on its way working up. The trout-fisher who understands her craft practises, therefore, throwing as light a line as possible, especially for brook fishing. If you are fishing deep still water, as on a lake (by *still* I mean not the actively running water of a stream), so long as there is a heavy breeze on, a rough line will not so much signify; but as all the most artful and delicate of trout-fishing takes place in the clearest water of very little depth, where if you have quick eyes you can see the trout lying, it is necessary to throw not only a delicate line, but also, if necessary, to be able to manage the process on your hands and knees—for if the trout catches the smallest glimpse of the fisherman (and his eyes are as sharp as needles), there is not the smallest chance of his letting himself be lured out of that pool for hours to come. Hence the advantage of wading up stream like an otter, as there is far less chance of the trout seeing you than if you advance along the bank above him. Patience, alertness of mind and eye, indifference to being wet, and good tools will help you to acquire an art which, though difficult, as is everything that is worth learning, will repay you a hundredfold. I have but one word to add: If you want to derive the utmost enjoyment in fishing a promising mountain stream, *fish alone*. A companion is a useless incumbrance to the true worshipper of the noble art of trout-fishing.

BOATING AND SCULLING

BY MISS A.D. MACKENZIE

A.D. MACKENZIE grew up at Henley-on-Thames. The family home, Fawley Court, was on the regatta course there, and her father (a barrister and Conservative candidate for Reading) served as a steward of the Henley Regatta for over sixty years. The family's luncheon parties during the boat races were advertised in the press.

Perhaps of all outdoor amusements rowing is one of the healthiest for ladies, besides being one of the most enjoyable. Just at first, of course, learning to row is rather tiring, but very soon one will find how far one can go without feeling any fatigue. For a girl who is learning, the great thing is to have some one who can row well to tell her all about it; and then, if she will only row bow and keep her eyes on stroke's back—without looking round every minute to see what her oar is doing—she will find she will soon get on. The great secret, of course, in rowing is not to dip the oar too deeply in the water, but merely to cover the blade, and then pull it well towards one. In going forward one ought to feather one's oar an inch above the water, and get well forward before taking another stroke.

Sculling is really quite as easy, if not easier, than rowing; and though at the start a beginner finds the sculls are apt to get rather unmanageable, still, after a little practice, she will much prefer it. Rowing is more one-sided than sculling, and the latter is naturally the better exercise, as both arms have a freer motion than in rowing. But, above all things, one should remember that the stretcher is made for use, not ornament, and that one cannot use it too much. So many ladies make the great mistake of merely rowing with their arms, when, if they only knew it, they would save themselves half the labour by bending forward, and bearing on the stretcher, in pulling each stroke.

It is essential for every English girl to learn to row, and no one can say anything against a lady rowing—though, of course, there are "some folks" who would run down anything that a lady does in the way of athletic exercises, more for the sake of argument than anything else. Twenty years ago it was very different: it was not considered *comme il faut* for a lady to row, and she never dreamt of doing so. Now, however, that everything is changed, it is clearly to be seen that it is the very best thing for her, and affords an amusement that, having once gone in for, she would be very sorry to give up.

Living nearly all the summer by the river gives one many opportunities of observing the river world, and it is often remarked that ladies know as much about managing a boat as men. On the Thames, between Cookham and Wargrave, ladies have for some time indulged in a great deal of rowing. At the former place, a few years ago, a ladies' eight was started, and the crew were all well trained, and kept good time, etc. At the Wargrave Town Regatta ladies have this last year or two come very much to the fore. Double-sculling and punting races have been competed for by them with much success. A gondola this year at Henley Regatta, pioneered by a lady, went along well, and kept clear of the other boats. A ladies' eight was also to be seen paddling up and down, and the rowers here again seemed proficient in the art. Last year there appeared at Marlow Regatta an eight which had come about seven miles down the river, and had been successfully steered through crowded locks; and the rowers looked none the worse for the long pull.

Ladies who are not adept on the water should not attempt to go out alone in boats and punts. This year at "Henley" three most beautifully "gowned" ladies appeared in a punt, and, as every one knows, a punt is, for an amateur, a by no means easy thing to manage. The three fair occupants found themselves, after they had tried for some time unsuccessfully to move along, struggling in the water, with the punt gaily floating away! They had had quite enough of the river by the time they were helped and pulled on to *terra firma*; and it was thought then by a good many who saw their deplorable condition that this would be a lesson to them for the future. But, alas! how perverse human nature is. The following day the same thoughtless three were again in their punt, running into the other boats with the sweetest unconcern, and evidently enjoying themselves very much.

Our English summers are so short and uncertain now that it is not always easy to find a day for an excursion on the river. It is by no means an uncommon sight to see a gaily-dressed party starting off in the highest spirits, to come back, a few hours later, drenched and depressed, with the cushions of the boat perched up in various ways to afford shelter to the occupants.

But why will some people go on the river fashionably attired? They look so much nicer and cooler and smarter in plain serge skirts and cotton shirts: only the latter should most certainly be fresh and clean, not tumbled and crumpled, looking as though they had been worn every day and in all weathers from the beginning of the boating season!

This summer I went off for a picnic on the river in a large heavy family boat, packed pretty closely. At starting, every one was volunteering to row, and there were numerous young lady beginners all most keen to show off their knowledge. Coming home, however, we were overtaken by a storm of rain when a long way from any sheltering trees. The two lady rowers quite collapsed at the first raindrops, and entangled their oars, and caught crabs, and were quite unable to continue rowing! There was not one of the huddled-up mass in the stern of the boat at all willing to take their places. Meanwhile the rain came down in torrents, till the boat inside was soaking, and little pools and rivers were coursing along the bottom of it. At last a middle-aged lady and one of the men volunteered their services—they had at starting quite led us to suppose that they were first-rate rowers. The lady was bow, and stroke, seizing the sculls in a business-like way, began. He placed them flat on the water, and then with an "Are you ready?" went suddenly forward, and shot back, feathering his oars through the water, and coming into violent collision with bow's sculls. Meanwhile, bow was chopping her oars up and down in a sharp decisive manner, without pulling them through the water at all. It need hardly be added that it was long, with this style of rowing, before we gained a place of shelter, arriving in by no means such an amicable mood as when we started.

But river picnics are undoubtedly great fun, and damp sticks for the fire and spiders in the tea-cups only add to the amusement. It is often at these picnics that the best oars grow suddenly lazy, and prefer sitting in the bows and being rowed to showing off their own skill. Steering a family boat requires no small amount of patience, as amateur oars find great pleasure in putting a lot of blame on cox, when they find the boat will not go as fast as they would like. It is much easier to learn to row in a heavy boat, as then, however much you move about, or however many crabs are caught, there is no fear of upsetting, and afterwards a light boat will be found a pleasant change.

CRICKET

BY LADY MILNER

LADY ADELINE GERTRUDE DENISON MILNER
(1859–1902) was one of eight ladies who founded
the first female cricket club in England in 1887, the
White Heather Club of Nun Appleton. It survived
until 1957, and its scorecards are now kept at Lord's.

What endless discussion and variety of opinion this subject has evoked! It has drawn down on our sex the most adverse criticism and scornful jeers; but then, on the other hand, we have been nobly and ably defended by those most competent to judge. Every day we find prejudice yielding to common sense, cricket for ladies becoming more and more popular; and now those who at one time hid their light under a bushel, and played in secret, have suddenly awakened to find themselves famous. It seems to me slightly inconsistent that many fathers and mothers should object to their daughter playing in cricket matches, who would not in the least object to that same daughter playing hockey on the ice; though in the one case she would only be playing with those of her own, and—let us say—gentler sex, while in the other case she would be playing mostly, if not entirely, with men and boys, the latter of whom are, as a rule, certainly not celebrated for much consideration, either of sex or *physique*, in the heat and excitement of the game. Then, again, if the anxious parent is a little afraid of her daughter indulging in the dangerous pastime of flirtation, and mixing up a little sentiment with the intricacies of the game, surely she can have no better protection than the other twenty-one ladies and the isolation of her position in the field required by the rules of cricket!

Far be it from me to disparage hockey, for I have spent many a happy day on the ice myself; but I think, as regards outdoor games for ladies, cricket should stand very high in the list, and the many distinctions drawn are, in my opinion, without a difference, unless it be to the advantage of cricket. It ought also to teach many things beyond the technicalities of the game, that will stand the player in good stead when cricket is a thing of the past; perseverance, endurance, courage, and self-control are all brought into play at cricket, and many things are to be learnt there which, if learnt properly, will fit us well for the battle of life. And then what fun it all is! Everybody likes an outing, and what can be more exhilarating than to start for a day's cricketing on a glorious summer morning, with your team in the highest of spirits, all bent on "death or glory," to one of those lovely old homes of England, where it is a pleasure merely to bask under the shade of some ancient tree, and where almost the only modern things to be found are the lady cricketers themselves? Then the chaff, the laughter, and the lunch, where each eleven invariably sit on opposite sides of the table, taking furtive stock of each other, or you survey sternly the bold damsel *vis-à-vis* who had the temerity to remove you from the wicket, perhaps when you had only just arrived there. It is true, the return home may be under more depressing circumstances; you may be gnawed by the demon of remorse at the thought of the pair of spectacles which is all that can be placed to your account, or you may sorrowfully wonder what on earth possessed you to drop that catch, upon the success of which nearly everything depended; but after all it is only a game, and you have had a great deal of pleasure in a short space of time, and you will soon "perk up" quite ready to start again, feeling perfectly certain that you will make your fifty—next time.

Now let us think a little about batting, which is certainly the most enjoyable part of the game, even if our innings, like many things of this life, are apt to be so short, although so sweet. We play rashly instead of steadily, and think more of making hits than of keeping our wicket up. It is a good rule to make, never to hit at a straight ball, tempting though it may be, until you are well set, and feel that you have mastered the cunning of the bowler. Play the balls carefully with a straight bat, the left elbow well forward, and keep your hits for a nice ball to leg or a long-hop to the off. These balls are the batswoman's delight, for being off the wicket they are perfectly safe to hit, and even if you miss them they can't bowl you out; so hit them, and hit them with all your might, and you will make a valuable addition to the score, besides experiencing a sensation of the keenest pleasure. Two of the principal rules to recollect in batting are, *never* to move the right foot, and to keep the left elbow and shoulder well forward. The first of these rules requires a great deal of practice to carry out thoroughly, and beginners will find that their first impulse on receiving a ball will be to lift the right foot,——preparatory, I suppose, to flight,——for it requires a certain amount of courage to stand up with unwavering front to a ball which you feel convinced is going to hit either your head or your legs.

I have heard sometimes of boys, who are being schooled in the rudiments of cricket, having their right foot pegged down in order to prevent the possibility of moving it, so important is this considered. Of course, as in every rule, there are exceptions, notably when you wish to cut a ball. In order to perform this feat you must step right across the wicket with your right foot, hitting the ball when it is exactly opposite the said foot; it requires a certain amount of strength in the wrists for this stroke, besides great accuracy of eye to time the ball, and take it at exactly the right moment. Very few ladies can cut well, but it is a wonderfully pretty stroke, and commands the greatest admiration. Perhaps it would be well to mention here that the "off" side is on the batsman's right, and the "leg" and "on" side on the batsman's left; and this latter is the side to which lady players are most partial, often committing the fault of "pulling" a ball round to their favourite spot. This is a grave mistake, as in the first place you are much more likely to miss it altogether by attempting this *coup*; and, secondly, you ought always to try and send the ball in the direction from which it came; that is to say, that if a ball is bowled to the off try and return it in that direction, and if a ball is bowled to leg, then, and then only, you may indulge yourself by hitting it to leg; but you will find, if you play with a perfectly straight bat, watching the ball most carefully from the moment it leaves the bowler's hand, and never forgetting to keep the left elbow forward, that you will almost involuntarily send it where it ought to go. Of course there are first-rate players, complete masters of the bowling, who frequently "pull" a ball in order to place it exactly where the fields are not; but I strongly advise my sisters-in-cricket—to the humble beginners of which only I venture to address myself—never to attempt this piece of daring, which would be put down entirely to ignorance on your part, and which would lose its point completely, for any captain who has studied ladies' play at all would invariably place most of her fields on the "leg" and "on" side. There is also another danger in trying to "pull" a straight ball to leg—you miss it, it does not miss you, it hits you on the leg, and you run a great risk of being given out "leg before wicket."

Then there is another important thing to remember, which is to try and get *over* the ball with your bat, not to let it run up the bat, which may result in your sending a tiresome little catch, almost impossible to miss. Endeavour to get on the top of the ball, and to send it along the ground as much as possible, and you will avoid the many woman-traps laid out to catch the unwary. When you make up your mind to hit, open your shoulders, and hit with all your strength; the little nervous pokes ladies are wont to indulge in is a frequent cause of their dismissal from the wicket. Either play a ball or hit it, but don't make a sort of "mongrel" stroke, which is neither one thing nor the other. Let me advise you also not to play with too heavy a bat. Of course the length of the bat you require depends very much on your height; but I do not think any lady requires a bat heavier than 2lbs. 2 ozs. The difficulty is to choose a light bat which will at the same time "drive"; but about this you can always get advice if you enlist the services of a male cricketing friend. On the whole, as regards batting, I think we shall not go far wrong if we unfailingly bear in mind these three rules: Play with a straight bat; keep your left elbow forward; let your right foot be immovable.

It seems to me, in my slight experience, that where ladies are most deficient is not so much in batting as in bowling. Many ladies are fair batswomen, but very few bowl well; and this is always the great difficulty in arranging an eleven. I think it is principally from want of practice, and also from the idea that if you can bat well nothing else matters much. This is the greatest possible mistake, for a good "all-round" cricketer—which adjective is not in this case a term of opprobrium applied to the lady's figure, but means a cricketer who is equally good in batting, bowling, and fielding—is a treasure rarely to be found, and is valued accordingly. These are the players who, to make up a strong eleven, are sought by the captain. Such are preferred infinitely to a brilliant creature who may be a splendid hitter, making mid-on tremble in her shoes, but who at the same time, by an unlucky mischance, may be rendered practically useless for the rest of the day, for if she can bat *only*, once she is out she is of no further use.

So that when you are learning cricket do not neglect your bowling. Of course some people are born bowlers, but still it is wonderful how much can be done by practice; and the best way to set about this is to put up a net behind the wicket, placing a mark about ten feet from the stumps, and bowl away steadily every day, striving to pitch your ball upon it. Do not bowl for too long at a time; the instant you feel tired leave off and rest, remembering always that the pace of the ball does not matter nearly so much as the pitch; a slow well-pitched ball does infinitely more damage than a fast badly-pitched one. Many ladies ruin their bowling utterly by trying to bowl too fast and too far. Twenty-one yards between the wickets, or even twenty, is quite far enough for ladies' bowling, and this stipulation ought always to be made in arranging a match. The ball gives most trouble to the "striker" when it pitches in the block hole. This sort of ball is called a "Yorker," and it lures many a batswoman to destruction by appearing to her as a half-volley, and it is only when she has fought the air in vain, and hears the death-rattle of the bails behind her, that she recognises the character of this fatal

Lorelei; therefore, my fellow-bowlers, if you would excel, perfect yourself in the "Yorker."

Fielding, too, is a very weak point in ladies' cricket, and yet it is so essential to success, and when well done so pretty to see. I think ladies fail especially in this particular, partly because they dare not stand up to a fast ball, and also because they think some one else will get it if they don't; and while they are looking round for that some one to do the work they ought to be doing themselves, the ball has passed them, and is over the boundary, and they have only their own cowardice and dilatoriness to thank for it. Then, what heart-breaking work it is for the bowler, when she is bowling her best for catches, to see those same catches being dropped here, there, and everywhere, all over the place; or how discouraging it is when—to save every run being of importance—the captain sees an easy ball going straight between the field's legs, and a three is added to the adversary's score, which at most ought only to have been a one. To field well you *must* get down to the ball. You must bend, and field it with *both* hands if possible, keeping your heels well together and your hands almost on the ground. A favourite form of fielding with some ladies is to stop the ball with their pet-ticoats. This may achieve their purpose, but it is, to say the least of it, most ungraceful, and is very bad "form," provoking a good deal of laughter among the spectators, and probably a remonstrance from their captain, who nat-urally does not like to see any one of her team doing anything so unworthy of real cricket. Watch anxiously every ball that is bowled, and be ready for it as if each one were coming straight to you, and you alone; when it goes to another field, anywhere in your line of action, mind you are ready to back her up, and to remedy any mistake she may make. Many an extra run has been saved by the field attending carefully to this rule. When you have to run to overtake a ball run as if for your very life, pounce on it as surely and truly as a hawk on her prey, and return it to the wicket-keeper in the twinkling of an eye. It is only given to very few of us to throw really well, for this is essentially a natural gift; but at any rate we can hurry up, and not dawdle about with the ball in our hand, or keep it a moment longer than is necessary.

To keep wicket is about the most difficult position in the field, and I will not even attempt to describe the various requirements necessary to fulfil this post satisfactorily; one thing, however, I will mention, and this is, to remind the wicket-keeper to stand close behind her wicket, ready to receive the ball thrown in to her from the field. The bowler must do likewise, as it might equally be thrown in to her end, and the nearest field must never fail to back up at each end, in order to prevent runs being made by an overthrow. However, whether we can throw well or not, let us at any rate try to remedy the great defect in our fielding, which is always the same, namely, that we will not stoop enough, and stoop we must in order to conquer.

Whatever decision the umpire gives you must implicitly acquiesce in outwardly. We may swear inwardly as much as we like, but if we are given out, out we must go. Ladies are proverbially fond of the last word, but on this occasion only we must waive our privilege, and accept the umpire's decision as final, for nothing spoils the enjoyment and harmony of a match more than angry disputing at the wicket, ending in utter discord and general unpleasantness for everybody. The captain also deserves your heartiest co-operation, for she has sometimes a hard time of it. There is always more or less difficulty in getting up a good team of lady-players, and just when she is congratulating herself on having done so, perhaps at the very moment when she is about to start, some one throws her over quite unjustifiably, merely penning an apologetic note, saying, "It looks so like rain I dare not venture to play cricket," or, "I feel so fatigued after the ball last night I would prefer to stay quietly at home." Certainly she ought to have stayed at home—but from the ball, not from the cricket match. The poor captain tears her neat head of hair in despair, and wonders wildly how she can conjure up a female cricketer out of empty space. I remember one occasion, when this had occurred, being short of one lady. We had to hunt about in highways and byways, trying to collect something in the female shape to come to our rescue, and make up our number. We suddenly heard a rumour that the butcher's daughter in the village had once handled a bat. We immediately rushed to her and implored her help; she very good-naturedly abandoned her chops for cricket, and so well did she use the fine pair of arms with which Nature had endowed her, wielding the willow with the same energy and success with which she had hitherto handled the cleaver, that she proved a most valuable addition to our side, and a real help in time of need.

I don't think any article concerning ladies would be quite complete without a word on that all-important subject of dress. We are told the tailor makes the man, and I suspect the dressmaker helps the woman—a good deal too; but let us, when we think of our appearance, think also of our comfort, for it is certain that we cannot give ourselves thoroughly up to the enjoyment of the game if we are thinking all the time how to help tumbling over our flounces or bursting our bodices. To be comfortable, we need not be dowdy; neither, on the other hand, need we appear on the field dressed as if for Ascot. Frills, furbelows, and feathers ought never to be seen at cricket, for anything of this sort looks out of place. Above all, let us not spoil our freedom of movement by encasing ourselves in steel armour, more commonly called "the correct corset"; though this word I mention with bated breath, and with a humble apology to any masculine reader whose eye may happen to stray over these pages. But so much of our success in this game depends on our quickness of movement and suppleness of body, that surely I may be pardoned for pointing out that if we are steel-bound and whalebone-lined throughout, the free use of our limbs which the game demands is rendered impossible; therefore in your pursuit of a ball let there not be ominous creakings of whalebone and splitting of side seams to delay your onward flight. Neither should

you ever forget to fasten your hat on securely.
So many ladies omit to do this, and it is no
uncommon thing to see a lady holding her hat
on with one hand, striving to catch a ball with
the other, and succeeding in doing neither.
Again, if you are fielding, and your hat falls off
and gets mixed up with the ball, the confusion
between you, your hat, and the ball obviously
creates great difficulties in fielding well, and
you may even, by an unfortunate mischance,
return your hat to the wicket-keeper instead
of the ball! Boots, I think, are a good deal
better for cricket than shoes, for the ball has
a playful habit of bumping about your ankles,
and boots in this case protect your feet a good
deal better than shoes. Whichever you wear,
however, have two or three spiked nails put
in before you go on to the cricket field. There
can be no more becoming or neat attire for
cricketing than a white flannel skirt, walking
length, a well-cut white shirt, a girth belt,
and a white sailor hat, with a ribbon and tie
of your club colours. This get up, if well car-
ried out, looks most smart and workmanlike,

and shows off a good figure to the greatest advantage; so, ladies, do not be afraid to don these garments, and you will be well dressed, because you will be suitably dressed.

It is always easier to preach than to practise. I have done the first; now you, dear ladies, must do the second, and may you derive as much pleasure from it all as I have. Cricket and summer are synonymous terms, and there is intense enjoyment to be found in both; so

> *"Let us laugh and be glad*
> *While the long sunny hours may last;*
> *Time soon enough to be sad*
> *When 'Cricket' and Summer are past."*

ARCHERY

BY MRS. C. BOWLY

It is not known when MRS. C. BOWLY was born
and died, but she was a serious and successful archer,
whose victories were mentioned more than once in
The Times at the end of the nineteenth century.

Ladies from an early period have been fond of Archery, for we see by a drawing in a manuscript of the fourteenth century that a lady has shot a deer, or wounded it, very adroitly. It was usual, when they shot, for the beasts to be confined in large enclosures, and driven in succession from the coverts to the stands where the fair sportswomen were placed. It is said of Margaret, the daughter of Henry VII, that on her way to Scotland a hunting party was arranged for her amusement in Alnwick Park, where she killed a buck with her arrow. It is not mentioned if the long or the cross bow was used on this occasion. We know that ladies shot with both, for when Queen Elizabeth visited Lord Monticute at Cowdrey in Sussex in 1591, "Her Highness tooke horse, and rode into the Park at eight o'clock in the morning, where was a delicate bowre prepared, under the which were Her

Highness musicians placed; and a cross bow, by a nymph, with a sweet song, was delivered into her hands, to shoote at the deere; about some thirty in number were put into a paddock, of which number she killed three or four and the Countess of Kildare one."

An old ballad about Robin Hood says of his followers that

> *"With them they had an hundred bows,*
> *The strings were well ydight;*
> *An hundred shefe of arrows good,*
> *With hedes burnish'd full bryght,*
> *And every arrow an ell long,*
> *With peacock well ydight;*
> *And nocked they were with white silk.*
> *It was a semely syght."*

Archery, by those who know nothing about it, is said to be "a game of the past," and "only interesting as a survival of an old English pastime"; but I do not think these would say so if they happened to be present on the Ladies' Day, on the Royal Toxophilite ground, in

Regent's Park, where on a bright July afternoon about a hundred ladies from all parts of England may be seen competing for the handsome prizes so liberally provided by the gentlemen belonging to that Society.

Very fortunate do those ladies feel themselves to be who receive an invitation, and many thoughts are given to the weather; for being used in winter by the Skating Club, the ground is apt to be damp after rain, but for the same reason it is the most perfectly level ground you can find to shoot on; in fact, it is said to spoil you for ordinary ranges.

Archery has certainly not been so fashionable since lawn tennis came into vogue. It does not give that violent exercise that our young people seem to enjoy; but those who have once taken to it are very reluctant to give it up.

There is so much to recommend it. You can practise alone, or with as many friends as you can persuade to join you; and, besides, it has this great advantage, that however badly you shoot it does not in the least affect others. It is healthy, and gives a moderate amount of exercise without being too fatiguing. Then there is no reason to give it up because you think you are growing too old; for grandmothers can shoot quite as well, and in some cases much better, than the younger generation; in fact, it is scarcely ever too late to begin. An old gentleman once remarked to my husband that he had begun archery rather late in life; and my husband quite agreed with him when, on inquiry, it appeared that he commenced at the age of seventy.

Some people object to archery as being "so expensive," but after the first start you rarely require anything more than a few arrows occasionally, and the number of these depends on how unlucky you may be in breaking or losing them. The distance a lady has to walk, in shooting the usual round of seventy-two arrows with a gentleman practising at eighty yards, is only about a mile and a quarter, or, if with ladies only, it is reduced to under a mile.

The best plan is to have a ground as near to the house as possible, and to have the targets always out, so that it should never be a question, "We have so little time, is it worth while to have them put up?" Good targets are a pleasure to shoot at, but bad targets, or any that can be left out of doors, are better than nothing. I have even heard it said that it is good practice to shoot at a piece of paper on the ground, as the real object is to learn to aim, and to be steady. In shooting with a rifle the powder or motive power is always the same; but in the case of the bow and arrow the powder is your draw and loose, which vary considerably, and your bow arm may be said to represent the stock.

Before I began shooting I was given a little pamphlet called "Position Drill," reprinted from the "Archers' Register." It contained many useful hints. I remember one was to stand before a looking-glass, so as to see if you were in the correct position, with right elbow, arm, hand, and arrow all in a straight line, the right hand under the right eye, and level with the chin. It is best to find a place that does not alter, and then always draw to the same spot. In days gone by they used to draw to the ear, or the collar-bone; but it is now thought that you aim better by having the fingers with the nock of the arrow directly under the eye; some shut one eye, others use both. I believe either is right.

The proper position when shooting is an easy and graceful one; but occasionally one sees such attitudes as almost recall the Statue of the Laocoon. As Roger Ascham quaintly remarked in 1545, "All the discommodities which ill custome hath grafted in archers can neyther be quycklye poulled out, nor yet sone reckened of me they be so manye... Some shooteth his head forwarde, as though he woulde byte the mark, and another stareth with hys eyes, as though they shoulde flye out; another winketh with one eye, and looketh with the other... Another will stand poyn-tinge his shafte at the marke a good whyle, and by and by he wyll gyve a whip and awaye, or a man wite. Another maketh suche a wrestling with his gere as though he were able to shoote no more as long as he lyued;" and he concludes a long and very amusing list with the very true remark, "And these faultes be eyther in the drawynge or at the loose, with many other mo which you may easelye perseyue, and so go about to avoyde them."

The subject of aiming is rather a difficult one; but I am sure that every one should have some fixed point at which to aim, and know where that is, so as to be able to alter it should occasion require, such as a strong wind with or against you, and many other circumstances that you learn by experience. This point will very much depend upon the archer's loose and the strength of her bow. There is no better point for an aim than the gold, but there are few who can use it, because they would either shoot too high or too low. Supposing, for instance, that all the arrows went over the target, then you must take a lower point, even if it be on the ground, until you get the arrows to hit about the centre of the target, and of course do just the reverse should they fly too low. If you aim at the gold at sixty yards, at fifty yards you will have to aim much lower; that is, if you use the same bow, for some people use a weaker one at the shorter distance, and thus always keep their aim at the same point.

Experienced archers tell beginners not to trouble so much about hitting the target as shooting a good arrow, that is, one that flies smoothly with no wavering motion. No doubt this is good advice, but, like advice in general, is not usually taken, as it is pleasant to do both, and hits lead you on to try for more; and every one knows there is nothing so encouraging as success.

A most important point in shooting is to keep your left arm steady, and, if possible, in the same position for a moment after the arrow has flown. Stand upright, with your feet firmly planted on the ground, not close together, but about six inches apart, left hand facing the target in front, the right below the one behind you, the bow grasped in a steady clasp, and in such a position that the string on being loosed does not hit the arm-guard, as this will take away from the force of the shot; to prevent this the lower knuckle of the thumb ought to be in a line between the middle of the handle and the string.

Care should be taken not to overdraw, that is, to draw the arrow beyond the handle of the bow, for by doing so you would probably break the arrow, and injure yourself. It should be drawn up to the end of the wood, leaving the point of the iron beyond the bow, and when fully drawn up, should be held just long enough to get a steady aim, for if held too long you will probably unsteady yourself, and it is also bad for the bow. The arrow is held between the first and second fingers, and the bow is drawn with either two or three fingers; and to prevent the string from hurting them "tips" or thimbles of leather are worn, or gloves with thick pieces of leather on the ends.

I think it a mistake only to shoot on "perfect days," for if you get a wind on the day of a public meeting—and my experience does not always point to the best weather at such times—how can you make a score at all if you have never shot in a wind before, and do not know how it will affect the arrow? A cold day, too, seems to make the arrow fly further, or one is oneself stronger, which gives the same result. Many new clubs are starting up now, and delightful afternoons they afford, giving no trouble to the hostess, as by three o'clock she knows how many will require tea, and all that she has to provide. Besides tea, there are the targets and ground; and she can then be sure that her guests are perfectly happy, and require no additional entertainment.

The four dozen arrows at sixty yards are usually shot before tea, and afterwards the two dozen at fifty yards, which always seem to be very quickly over, and to end only too soon.

In Herefordshire and Worcestershire, and possibly in other counties, they have very big entertainments, including an early dinner, and often ending with a dance for those who like to stay for it; but I am now only speaking of the usual country clubs. To form one of these is quite an easy matter. You call a few of your friends together—the more enthusiastic the better—choose a small committee, and make a few rules, which can easily be copied from those of some other club; decide as to the entrance fee and subscription, and where to hold the meetings, either at one another's houses or on a convenient public ground, and all is done. One rule should always be observed—to begin at a fixed time, and wait for no one; if you once begin to wait there is an end to the punctuality of your members.

Then the bows and arrows must be purchased. Do not buy too strong bows at first— about twenty-five pounds, unless you are very strong, is quite heavy enough for a beginner, and a lancewood bow is good enough. A yew bow can be bought later, when you know what strength you require, as they are expensive.

How well I remember our first meeting! We had been asked to join the new club, and so doubtful were we of ever being able to shoot, that we hesitated as to whether we should not begin by being honorary members, and only act the part of spectators. However, we decided to start as shooting members, so I bought some arrows, borrowed a bow, received some hints from a friend, and set forth for the rendezvous in great trepidation, fervently hoping I might not make myself positively ridiculous. And here I may say, for the encouragement of those equally faint-hearted, that in the following year I succeeded in winning the second prize at the Grand National Archery Meeting. That day, however, I made, from the four dozen arrows at sixty yards, 8 hits, 24 points; only a very small result, but one with which I was more gratified than I am now, if I do not miss the target with any of the forty-eight arrows, and make between two and three hundred points with them. We never began the fifty yards, as the rain put a stop to our shooting for that day. No doubt my style was rather peculiar, for I knew nothing about "form" in those days; but I read up a good book on archery, and we started a ground and targets of our own. By the end of the season the recruits had greatly progressed, and these, added to the little nucleus of veterans, formed quite a respectable club. Some of our then beginners now attend the public meetings, and we have others coming on who bid fair to do us credit in the future.

The Grand National Archery Meeting is the great public event of the year. It was first held at Knavesmire, near York, in 1844. No ladies shot that year, but in the following year eleven ladies came to the targets, only shooting at sixty yards; and they do not appear to have attended in any numbers until 1851, when their shooting was considered to be very good. The score of the championess of that year was five hundred and four, whereas in 1891 the present championess, Miss Legh, made seven hundred and ninety-eight; in fact, the former score would not now secure even a sixth-score prize, so greatly have the ladies improved.

The champion and championess are chosen from the result of the two days' shooting; and, besides the badge and bracer, and the valuable money prizes that are given, the first four have gold (silver-gilt), and the two next silver medals. These are score prizes, and upon their reverse is engraved the motto of the society, "Union, True Heart, and Courtesie." The winners of all the other prizes have brooches.

For the match between the counties there are also six challenge brooches, which are held by the six ladies composing the winning county team. Gloucestershire has won these for the last four years.

At this meeting every one shoots on even terms; but the successful competitors are required to allow certain deductions from their score at all other public meetings. Thus, the championess has to give 25 per cent.; the second person, 20 per cent.; the third and fourth, 15 per cent.; the fifth and sixth, 10 per cent.

The first meeting of the season is that of the Midland Counties, held at Leamington in June— a very pleasant beginning—and it is followed by the Crystal Palace, the Great Western, and the Great Northern. They all, excepting the Crystal Palace, have championesses of their own, and bracelets, belts, and badges for the holders. Any one may attend by paying the entrance fees, and although most of the good shots go, they are so handicapped that a fair chance of a prize is given to others. All who can ought to attend them. A beginner is always welcomed most kindly, and hints are given to those who desire them. There is also much to be learnt by watching the shooters, but it must be remembered that many good archers are not altogether free from faults or peculiarities; and, as Roger Ascham says, "Good mennes faultes are not to be followed." At the public meetings the ladies and gentlemen are placed at different targets, generally five at each; the third lady is appointed captain, and enters the scores, but there is always a gentleman as judge, who measures the golds, and settles any question that may arise. The colour an arrow has hit is often a nice point, as the slightest touch gives the archer the right to claim the higher ring in value; the rings count, commencing with the gold, 9, 7, 5, 3, 1. Three arrows are shot at each end, and should they all go into the gold every lady shooter gives a shilling to the fortunate owner of them, who sometimes, as on the Ladies' Day of the Royal Toxophilite Society, may get as much as £5. Two arrows are not unfrequently sent in, but when it comes to the third it is such nervous work, and requires such perfect steadiness, that it seldom finds its way there also.

The Ladies' Day, Royal Toxophilite Society, July 1893

The excuses made for bad shooting—and
even the best archer is liable to variations—
are always numerous, and often go far to prove
that archers are not deficient in the inventive
or imaginative faculties. Every one knows that
the fault often lies with themselves; yet the
blame must be placed somewhere else, and the
ingenuity with which this is done is sometimes
quite extraordinary. The ground, the wind,
the light, the weather, the state of health, and
many other excuses, are all reasonable enough,
for they often very much affect the shooting.
Even the excuse given by a lady for not shooting so well the second day of a meeting as on
the preceding one, that her furniture was then
being moved into another house, and that she
could not help thinking of how far they were
taking proper care not to injure it, may have
been a just one, for anything that disturbs the
mind is certainly detrimental; but when a lady
attributed her want of success to the anxiety
occasioned by the illness of a near relative,
and, on the sympathetic hope being expressed
that the invalid was a little better, replied,

"Oh, yes, thank you! she has been quite well for some months," the effect did seem rather remote from the cause, although of course the result of an old strain may last some time. The pettish remark, on missing the target, and with it a prize, "It was all owing to those people cackling behind me," when they were at some distance, would not, under the circum-stances, have been very severely criticised by her companions, even had it not been almost immediately followed, on hearing her excuse gravely repeated, by the smiling admission, "Oh, no, no! it was only this person" (pointing to herself) "who was to blame."

It is true, in this case, the complaint was too far-fetched; nevertheless, it does disturb you very much to have people talking close to you, perhaps telling some piece of interesting gossip, or even making remarks about, or to, yourself, just as you are on the very point of shooting.

In public meetings care is taken to prevent this, as every one is expected to keep some yards behind the person shooting, and they are, at the same time, rather solemn affairs; but in private clubs much greater laxity prevails.

At the critical moment of loosing the arrow the archer should have her whole mind and undivided attention fixed upon her shooting. Unfortunately, I know of no receipt to prevent worries or distracting thoughts that may present themselves at the most inopportune moment, but the interruptions I have alluded to may, and ought to, be avoided. The archer has, indeed, enough to occupy her whole attention, which may be illustrated by the remark of a lady who, on being asked why she was so long in shooting, said that "she was thinking over the twenty things it was necessary to take into account before she let off her arrow."

And now I must say something more on the subject of bows and arrows. There are various kinds of bows—self yew, two-piece bows, and lancewood. I prefer the self yew, to which is generally given the first place, and it is the most pleasant to shoot with: but some first-class archers prefer the two-piece bows;

Mrs. C. Bowly, Championess, 1893

perhaps yew-backed yew, or yew-backed hickory, or some other wood; it is said they shoot more evenly, and they have the advantage of being cheaper; but never having tried one, I do not feel competent to give an opinion. Being made of more than one piece of wood, there is more danger of such bows becoming unglued if exposed to damp. The bows composed of three pieces of wood are rarely now used by ladies.

The weight of a lady's bow varies from about twenty-two to thirty-two pounds; the "weight" is the strength of pull. A thirty-pound bow requires a force of thirty pounds to draw the middle of the string an arrow's length from the handle. If you find your bow too heavy, the bow-maker will always reduce it to any strength you wish; but this should not be done too hastily with quite a new bow, as *use* up to a certain point has the same effect, and a novice will find her arm get stronger with practice. I have heard it said that some ladies shoot in the summer to strengthen their arms and wrists for hunting in the winter.

A bow should not be left strung too long; but, at the same time, I am not in favour of too frequently unstringing, although Mr. Muir maintained that to unstring a bow at each end is as pleasant to the bow as to rest on a camp-stool is to the archer. It is usually thought sufficient to unstring after the long distance is shot, or when, from any cause, a pause takes place in the shooting. Bows are said, if used too much, to "tire" or weaken. Rest, however, may restore them to their former vigour if they have not been too persistently overworked. A hot day will also have the effect of reducing the strength of the bow, and an archer must take all this into account. The best arrows are made of pine, with a harder wood at the foot, and have peacock feathering—not the tail feathers, but the strong red ones from the wing. Their usual weight varies from 3 to 3·6, and occasionally 3·9, which is calculated on what they really weigh in silver coin; thus, 3·3 means three shillings and a threepenny piece.

As to dress, which is always an important consideration with ladies, it can, in this case, be left to your own inclination. Only wear something in which you feel perfectly free, and can comfortably stretch out and bend your arms; and choose a material which will not be spoiled by damp or even wet weather. Goloshes are useful on a damp ground, and a waterproof cloak, in which your arms are free, is quite a necessity for a public meeting, as the gentlemen seem to consider the rain over, and ring the bell to summon the ladies from their tent, when they are often not of the same opinion; and although you are supposed not to shoot in the rain, if a shower comes on, you have to wait until every one has shot before you can cross over and rescue your arrows. The said arrows are usually the greatest sufferers, as the feathers, being only glued on, will come off on being continually wet.

There is a certain fascination about archery that is quite incomprehensible to out-siders, who erroneously think that it must be a very dull amusement. We have not unfre-quently found that guests, who protested that they could never shoot, but would "just like

to try what it was like," have become so cap-
tivated by it that on their return home they
have started it on their own account. I never
saw a more striking instance than that of a
gentleman visiting at our house, who had
never been known to care for games, sports,
or athletic exercises of any kind, but who,
when we induced him just to take a few shots,
suddenly became so enamoured of it that,
leaving his beloved books and papers, he was
detected gliding off to the archery ground,
bow in hand, to indulge, as he thought, in a
little private practice. Only let the neophyte
experience the charm of hearing the thud on
the target of her own well-placed arrow, and
she is generally taken captive at once.

GOLF

BY MISS ALICE M. STEWART

Nothing certain is known of MISS ALICE M. STEWART, apart from this proof of her passion for golf.

The extraordinary craze for Golf among ladies which has developed within the last few years forms a remarkable feature in the history of the Royal and Ancient Game; and the fact that many ladies have shown great skill in the short game, as is proved by the excellence of their scoring in competitions open to both ladies and gentlemen, leads us to believe that those ladies who have had the advantage of learning to play as children on long courses will prove themselves no mean adversaries to the average golfing man, even on a long course.

The increasing popularity of the game may be due partly to the endless variety it affords, and also to the fact that it is played in the open air, in all weathers (except when snow is on the ground), and at all times of the year. The exercise it entails is not violent, as is the case with so many outdoor sports and games. No one who has ever wielded a club can forget the feeling of pleasure and pardonable self-satisfaction which was experienced by the sight of the clean-hit ball soaring into a wall of azure, a tiny, white speck in the far distance.

It is impossible to make a non-player believe that there is as much excitement in a good close match at golf, even to an interested spectator, as there is in a game of lawn-tennis, cricket, or any other popular pastime. Kingsley is right in saying that, if Cricket is the King of Games, Golf is certainly the Queen.

To the uninitiated it appears that the game consists in hitting a small ball as hard as possible, not at your opponent's head, which might cause some excitement, but anywhere out of sight; and then, with your hands in your pockets and a pipe in your mouth——(this is supposing the tussle to be taking place between two men, of course)——you proceed to look for the said ball, still paying no attention to your opponent, who is also probably out of sight, and who appears to be as indifferent to the result of the game as you are. No casual observer could possibly imagine that these seemingly callous individuals are in reality two smouldering volcanoes, ready at the smallest provocation—caused (maybe) by the tiniest breach of the strict etiquette of the game by the one, or by an unexpected piece of good luck happening to the other—to give strong proofs of the excitement which is there, though concealed under an outward aspect of the greatest nonchalance. So keen at any moment may become the discussion on some point of the game, that even the best of friends have, through playing in the same match, been parted for ever, and have even been known to decline to finish the one on which they happened to be engaged owing to a question of handicap, string, etc., arising, over which they could agree only to differ. Few will believe, until they have tried, how great is the strain on the nerves which this very suppression of outward excitement causes during several closely contested matches in tournaments or in medal play. The strongest man, under such conditions, may, in a couple of days, become a weak and nerveless being.

Is golf a game for ladies? Certainly; for if we go, even casually, into the history of the growth of ladies' golf, we shall find that it is not such a new craze as it appears—that for years ladies have been gradually learning the art and giving the game a fair trial. Had this trial been unsuccessful, the game would long ago have sunk into oblivion, and this question could never have arisen.

The game is hardly in its infancy; for though little interest in it was shown by the general public until quite recently, as far back as the year 1867 the Ladies' Golf Club in St. Andrews was started. As this Club holds quite a unique position, apart from its proud one of seniority, amongst the crowd of Ladies' Golf Clubs which have sprung up with mushroom-like rapidity, a few words on its early history may not be out of place here; the less so when we take into consideration that from this small centre, and from the carefully nurtured enthusiasm of years, has gone forth a small army of lady golfers, ready to spread their ardour, and to start new clubs, wherever the soles of their feet may rest. When the St. Andrews Club was started, a golfing lady was regarded by the matrons and steady-going individuals in the ancient city as something too terrible for words; and the hubbub among these good souls, caused by the announcement that the Club was actually started, would scarcely be credited nowadays.

A damsel with even one modest putter in her hand, on her way to the green, was looked upon as a fast and almost disreputable person, certainly as one to be avoided. I know not what they say now, when they meet one of the numerous enthusiasts of the long game on her way to the Links, with a sheaf of clubs nearly as large as herself. Such enthusiasts may be seen playing morning, noon, and night, in all weathers and with vigorous pertinacity, in spite of the outcry of man, and the horrified expressions of the aforesaid worthy ladies, of whom a few still remain, clinging with limpet-like tenacity to the rules of propriety laid down for them by their forefathers.

Their voices are, however, silenced for ever by the overwhelming majority in favour of healthful exercise for girls. A few are even beginning to admit that, as there is some good to be found in everything, so the fashion may be excellent and laudable which encourages the exercise of walking, the development of muscular action and strength, and the training of nerve, eye, and, I may add, temper.

The membership of the St. Andrews Ladies' Golf Club at its start was only one hundred; now its numbers have risen to upwards of six hundred, and more than one hundred members have started for the Autumn Competition for the Club Gold Medal, the prize most valued by those who win it, and most longed for by those who do not. To this latter category belong those misguided souls who imagine bad luck always pursues them through every competition——those whose nerves always give way at the critical moment, though for a week, beforehand, so they say, no one could possibly have beaten them. Then there are those who never will improve (though they practise daily for months without ceasing, and always play a fairly steady game), added to a host of keen putters, old, young, and middle-aged, good, bad, and indifferent, too numerous to mention.

The solace of the unfortunate many who cannot become the holders of scratch medals is in the handicap competition, and to the latter may be due some of the marvellous popularity of the game. Every club which numbers over one hundred members, or even fewer, ought to have an annual handicap competition, as well as its scratch competitions; and let us hope in the dim future the art of handicapping will be so perfect that every match will be halved, and every score handed in will be the same figure. How will the "coming race" legislate for such a state of affairs?

The course for ladies, as laid down at St. Andrews, differs in many respects from those started during the last few years at other places. The space of ground at the disposal of the club being limited, the holes are short, and members are only permitted to play with wooden putters. The hazards consist of the Swilcan Burn, over which the course does not go, but into which many an unwary golfer's ball is trapped by wind, and the unaccountable eccentricities of the player. Whin-bushes bristle round numerous holes, bunkers yawn near others, but the same remark applies to them as to the Burn. Across a footpath you must, however, play, and if an unlucky kick leave your ball in it, you have but small chance of securing even a half of the hole, should your opponent's ball have run safely over and be lying on the green. The turf is very short and fine, and, consequently, a very high standard of putting can be attained. The course being undulating, and very few of the greens level, a crafty, careful old hand can often hole impossible looking putts, which, the writer has been told, are not inaptly described by the Arab caddies as "snakers," so winding and wriggling may be the course of the ball before it finally disappears safely into the hole. It has often been remarked that the best putters on that green are also the best on any other.

But excellent as is this green in teaching the cunning of the art of putting, we must go to North Berwick for perfection in the long game. There the ladies boast of a golf course second to none, whereon they may play their driver, bulger, brassey, or iron shots at will. I hope, however, the day is not far distant when St. Andrews will have a course for ladies equal, if not superior, to any in the British Isles.

Let the novice remember that to be steady and deadly at putting is half the battle, and will inspire more fear in the heart of the opponent than the longest ball driven off the tee.

Never was a truer speech made by the old caddie than when discussing, with a kindred spirit, the play of a learned professor, for whom he had been carrying. He remarked that "Any one can do thae Greek and Latin, but it taks a man wi' a heid to play gowff." The head and the hand must work together, and constant careful practice is the only way to attain an average amount of skill. One of the finest golfers of the day, who was asked the secret of his accurate putting and splendid play, replied, "Just take an awful lot of trouble." Expressive, and very true!

But a word to those who begin to play on public links, where the course was originally intended and laid down for mankind. They should remember it is only natural they should be regarded as intruders——and intruders they certainly are——on those who have had the right of way, so to speak, for maybe forty years or more, and for whom the game was first of all designed; and they should consequently do their best to interfere as little as possible with the regular players.

Beginners should not forget that there are as strict rules laid down for the game of golf as for any other game. A book of the rules can be had for a few pence from any bookseller, and these rules should be carefully learned, as well as the bye-laws of the course on which the player sets out on her first attempts.

The etiquette, or unwritten law, of the game is difficult for a novice to comprehend. No one can blame a beginner for not playing well, but ignorance of the A B C of the game is quite unpardonable, and often leads to disagreeable encounters with old experienced players—encounters which would, in most cases, be easily avoided if a careful perusal of the rules were the first step towards learning the game, instead of, as is generally the case, one of the last. However unimportant the match may be, the rules of golf should be strictly adhered to; so that when playing in a competition, as many beginners do, no infringement of the rules would occur, and all unseemly wrangling would be avoided.

Beginners should ask the advice and help of a good and experienced golfer in selecting clubs. It is as difficult for the novice to know the good points of each club as for an inexperienced eye to recognise those of a horse. Begin with as few clubs as possible; you will more easily learn to handle others when you have become thoroughly at home with one or two. Do not invest in a long driver; with a short club you have more control over your swing.

After a careful selection of clubs, the next important thing is to stand properly and far enough away from the ball to allow the arms to be outstretched, and to swing easily and freely, not with the elbows tucked closely to the sides, as many beginners do. Follow up the stroke with the club after the ball is hit. If the circular motion of the club is suddenly discontinued, an erratic drive will be the result, off either the toe or the heel of the club.

It is a great mistake for ladies who are beginners to attempt a full swing until they have complete control over their movements, which is most unlikely in the early stages of the game. Even after a certain amount of proficiency is attained, an easy half swing, and the globe clean hit, will accomplish far more than a full or nearly full swing and the ball half missed.

A common mistake made by beginners is the roll of the body. It should be borne in mind that the swing should be with the arms and from the shoulders; the rest of the body should be kept steady, though not rigid and stiff. Some begin their drive by slowly lifting first one foot and then the other, till they have quite thrown themselves off their balance. Whilst this operation is proceeding, the club is stiffly and slowly raised according to the old adage "Slow back." This will never be followed by the other old adage, "Far and sure." I have never seen satisfactory results attending this method. I always feel a pang of sorrow about that style, too; because it is so painstaking, so careful, and so evidently the result of much thought and deliberation on the part of the performers. One is bound, therefore, to admit that it is hard lines when success does not crown their efforts. Avoid such a style; play with as much freedom of swing as you like, and not as if you were a waxwork figure wound up, which must slowly and laboriously go through certain movements.

Too much style is as bad a fault as too little. The excess of style cultivated by some players becomes ridiculous, because in doing so they lose all natural ease in playing, and, should any slight hitch in the routine of their method of play occur, they are as certainly unable to hit the ball as a waxwork figure, over-wound, or with a slight hitch in its internal mechanism, would be unable to continue its movements. But this natural ease is difficult to attain for those who do not begin as children. The advantage is enormous to those whose earliest efforts were with spade and potato in the back garden; and these will always hold their own in the long run against those whose game began at a certain age—which is difficult to define, but is long after the spade and potato have given way to a miniature set of clubs and a ball, and the back garden to a daily tramp round a long course.

Though it seems like putting the cart before the horse, I should strongly advise those who intend to play a good game, and not to be mere triflers in the art, to go through a severe course of "putting," till they are certain of laying dead any putt of eighteen feet, and never missing one of three; and for this practice the green at St. Andrews is invaluable. Another good way to learn to putt correctly is to practise at one hole, on a flat green, from which a double row of tees, about three yards apart, have been laid down, commencing at one yard from the hole, and increasing the distance yard by yard, until you are certain of holing in two strokes, at twenty yards from the hole.

With this skill attained, a solid foundation is laid on which to start the other varieties of play which occur in the long game. After a good beginning, let no one be discouraged by suddenly playing badly; it is only the natural result of ignorance of the elementary part of the game.

An untiring patience, good clubs, and a careful coach are the ingredients which, when they have been secured, will seldom fail to turn out a good golfer.

FENCING

BY LADY COLIN CAMPBELL

LADY COLIN CAMPBELL, the woman whose infamous divorce case (see "Trout-fishing") inspired one newspaper to say she had "the unbridled lust of a Messalina and the indelicate readiness of a common harlot," was born in 1857. In 1889, she became the first female editor on a London paper not exclusively aimed at women. Although shunned by good society, she was a successful writer and journalist, a member of The London Library, and died in 1911.

Amongst sports and pastimes Fencing perhaps is the only one that owes nothing of its absorbing fascination to the accident of surroundings. In my article on trout-fishing I have spoken of the all-important part surroundings occupy in that as in other sports. If you were asked to pull trout out of a tank, or to shoot stags in a stable-yard, you would decline indignantly, not only on account of the unsportsmanlike nature of such a proposal, but also on account of the boredom such a proceeding would entail. In every sport surroundings are the chief consideration. The open moorland, the sense of freedom, the beauty of Nature, the obstacles to be overcome, the trifling incidents with the dogs, or the missing pony with the luncheon-basket,—all these combine to create and maintain an interest in the particular sport you are following, and to invest it with a charm which is, though you may not be aware of it, far more lasting and potent than the mere fact, delightful as it is in the moment of success, of killing your prey, whatever it may be. But fencing is different. It owes absolutely nothing to any surroundings whatever. A good *salle d'armes* is an excellent thing, with its smooth floor, its comfortable lounges round the walls, its trophies of foils, duelling swords, masks, and gauntlets; but once you have your foil in your hand, and your opponent in his place before you, a strip of kamptulicon in a garret will afford you the opportunity of as great enjoyment as the most luxurious *salle* ever built.

In no other sport or pastime that I am acquainted with (and I may say I have tried my hand at most), is the interest so close, so intense, or so concentrated as in fencing. At other athletic sports, such as cricket, lawn-tennis, or golf, you have an adversary, it is true, but he is so far removed from you that in a sense he becomes almost impersonal; in fact, as regards the last-named game I am heretical enough to say that it seems to me you might just as well have no adversary at all. In fencing, on the other hand, you are in actual touch with your opponent; the delicate rod of steel in your grasp is a lightning-conductor that instantaneously flashes to your brain the knowledge of what attack your adversary is meditating, for the *sentiment du fer* should tell you what to do, even if your eyes were blindfolded. Every faculty of your brain, every muscle of your body, every nerve of eye and hand, are all on the alert; and you *live* more intensely, more vividly, in an "assault" of a quarter of an hour than most people do in a week.

What makes fencing so peculiarly appropriate to women is the fact that unusual strength is not only unnecessary, but is almost a drawback to proficiency in this great and serious art. Well-knit muscles can be gained in a comparatively short time, especially by the use of dumb-bells—or, still better, Indian clubs—every morning; and, for the rest, suppleness and agility can also be acquired to a certain useful extent by those not born of the panther-race, which has given all the great fencers to the world. For feline quickness is the most valuable of all gifts to the fencer—quickness of spring in advance or retreat; quickness of hand in disengagements (such as Hauteclaire Stassin's in D'Aurévilly's "Le Bonheur dans le Crime," "Qui vous arrivait au beau milieu de la poitrine comme une balle, même quand elle vous avait prévenu qu'elle allait dégager sur vous"); quickness of eye to see the breadth of a line when your adversary, in some too brusque *parade*, uncovers himself for the space of half a second, and receives the *coup droit*, which can be successful on such occasions only by lightning-like speed and precision; quickness of brain to judge at once of *le jeu* of your opponent, and to regulate your attack and defence accordingly. There is no such nerve tonic, no such bracing occupation as fencing; and one would hear considerably less of hysteria, of morphine-mania, and of other regrettable characteristics of *fin-de-siècle* existence, if women were to take to fencing as one of the regular occupations of their day.

The first and foremost necessity in setting to work is to provide yourself with a thoroughly good master, either French or Italian, according to which school of fence most attracts your sympathies. There are, no doubt, some good English fencing-masters who would train a pupil properly; but the delicacy of the fencing art, its total absence of physical brutality, is, as a rule, entirely foreign to the athletic aptitudes of an Englishman, to whom single-stick with its knock-down blows comes quite naturally. The chances are that you may hit upon an indifferent instructor, who will let you clash foils with him; will allow you to engage in an assault before you have taken lessons for six months; will permit you to contract every sort of bad habit and carelessness of attitude;——and at the end of several years of such fencing instruction you will be considerably surprised and chagrined to find, on going to a proper French *maître d'armes*, that you have to begin all over again, and will probably have to spend six months unlearning everything you have previously been taught.

I have been invited to see ladies fence here in London under the eye of their instructor; they had been sedulously at work for over a year, and they knew no more about the very alphabet of the art they were supposed to be fairly proficient in than a cat does of a case of pistols! The fault was not theirs, for they were full of righteous enthusiasm for the noble art of fence; but it made me wrathfully inclined to spit the instructor on one of his own foils for wasting and misdirecting such excellent raw material.

Once you have settled with your professor, the next thing is to provide yourself with a practical costume; and amongst the few women-fencers I have seen at work in this country I have remarked such absurdities in the way of garments, that a word on the subject may not be out of place. Freedom— absolute and entire freedom—of movement is a *sine quâ non* in fencing; if you feel yourself trammelled in any way, your attention is distracted from the work you have to do, and you do it badly,—than which it is far better not to do it at all. I have seen women fencing in serge bathing-dresses; anything more hideous and unpractical it would be hard to conceive: and so far from a fencing costume being necessarily hideous, it can be as distinctly graceful and becoming a dress as a well-made woman need wish to wear. But it must be practical above every other consideration, and with this end in view it is absolutely necessary to discard skirts. I have seen women fence in skirts to the knee; they were not only perpetually getting in their way when lunging and recovering quickly, but were in much worse taste than the wearers had probably any idea of. A pair of very full knickerbockers,* either buttoned or buckled with a band round the knee, or gathered there by an elastic, are far better in every way than a ballet-dancer's skirt. The jacket should be long and close fitting, the skirts reaching as far down the leg as the lunge will allow; it should be widely double

---

* The material should be fairly thick; the best to my mind being velvet corduroy, which should be lined throughout with either silk or linen.

breasted, and buttoned along the seam of the left shoulder, round the arm-hole, and down the side seam. It may be made of any material the fencer pleases—leather, corduroy, or canvas; and from the centre front seam round to the side seam under the right arm it must be heavily wadded, all over the chest and side, for protection from foil hits. Even this wadding for those who mean to fence seriously, and are sufficiently advanced for the free play of an assault, is hardly sufficient; and I, personally, have fine steel chain-mail placed between two folds of doeskin as interlining to my corduroy jacket.

Let it not be thought that in what I have said as to dispensing with skirts I advocate the burlesque-like dress of the *Escrimeuse* who figures on the wall of the Salle des Jeux at Monte Carlo; nor, much as I appreciate the grace of d'Aurévilly's literary dandyism, should I advise any *tireuse* to copy the costume of the Mdlle. Hauteclaire already alluded to, who is described as "lacée dans ce gilet d'armes de peau de chamois qui lui faisait comme une cuirasse, et les jambes moulées par ces chausses en soie qui en prenait si juste le contour musclé"; even the author himself doubts "si cela s'appelle vêtue." In the minor accessories, I recommend a mask fitted with a spring to hold the mask close to the head; a sort of "bib" in buck or chamois leather hanging from the chin of the mask completes the protection to the neck. To my mind, the ordinary gauntlet is over-padded, and resembles too much a boxing-glove, preventing the free play of fingers—the *doigté*—and of wrist. In touching shoes we step upon dangerous ground; there arises the vexed question of heels or no heels. Undoubtedly heels are in theory indefensible; practically, I fear that few *débutantes* in the *salle d'armes* will be willing at first to sacrifice the fine *cambrure* which the heel—that "bearing-rein of the foot," as it has been cleverly called—gives to the feminine instep; and for the comfort of the less philosophical of my sister-fencers I can only say that Mdlle. Louise Abbéma (herself, I believe, an artist in foils as well as colour), in her charming *croquis* of an *Escrimeuse* which appears in *L'Escrime Française*, has endowed her heroine's shoes with a pair of unmistakable heels. But when the fencer passes from the goose-step to the higher fencing evolutions, heels must be utterly and absolutely discarded.

In choosing foils I should advise lightness and balance (depending upon the mode of mounting) to be chiefly consulted. For ordinary use, No. 4 blades of Solingen or Klingelthal manufacture will perhaps be found best adapted to a woman's hand. And now let us imagine the *Escrimeuse* (the present poverty of our fencing language must excuse my frequent use of this word and of *Tireuse*) properly equipped, standing "on guard" before her adversary, or rather her fencing-master. What advice of the greatest use can I give her in the small compass allotted me? How is it possible in a few words even to touch upon the different positions of preparing for and coming on guard, and of the *développement*, as the subsequent transition from rest to action—comprising the thrust and lunge—is called?

On the latter I must be permitted to quote the words of Camille Prévost*:—

"However quick the development may be, it is indispensable that the extension of the arm should precede the movement of the body, since it is the hand which holds the foil, and it is with the hand the hit is made." A golden rule this to remember; and it may be observed that a woman, being, as a rule, light-handed, is less likely to rely upon the "athletic" shoulder, which is one of the great stumbling-blocks and blemishes in masculine fencing. Here, too, I might supplement Prévost's teaching by mentioning the importance—the absolute necessity—of the movement of the hand preceding the movement of the foot. Those who have, like myself, had the advantage of taking lessons

---

* A *maître d'armes*, who, as theorist and fencer, amply deserves the compliment paid him by Paul Bourget in the sonnet prefixed to the volume "L'Escrime et le Duel" (par C. Prévost et G. Jollivet in the "Bibliothèque du Sport"),—

> "Prévost, nul mieux que vous n'en garde le secret,
> Et vous avez fixé cet Art, où notre race
> Sut empreindre son don de mesure et de grâce
> D'une plume qui vaut votre savant fleuret."

from M. Philippe Bourgeois, will remember the infinite patience with which he time after time repeats the admonition, "Trop tôt le pied"; the reason being, that if the foot starts first the fencer "gives away" both himself and the secret of his attack.

Later on, the mysteries of "pronation" and "supination" (a less deadly use of feminine fingers "turned up or down" than that in vogue with the Roman dames at the gladiatorial shows), the four lines of engagement——the "high lines" and "low lines," will be revealed to the aspirant to fencing honours. At present they must remain as enigmatic as to modern fencers are

> *"The fincture, carricade, and sly passata,*
> *The stramazon and resolute stoccata,*
> *Wiping Mandritta, closing embrocata,*
> *And all the cant of the honourable fencing*
> *   mystery."*

Here I can do no more than say that the "*engagement*" is the junction of the foils, and that it may take place in every line, and derives the name of the *parade* (parry) from the position of the hand and the line which it occupies. It will soon fall to the "*tireuse*" to take her own line in the methods of attack and defence; and she will probably prefer, with the modern classical school of fencing, to affect especially *Quarte*, *Sixte*, *Tierce*, *Seconde*, and *Octave*, and leave to the more romantic and flamboyant fencers *Prime*, *Quarte volante*, *Quinte*, *Septime renversé*, and the *Flanconnade* dear to the great Angelo. If she follow my advice, she will use sparingly the *Coupé* (cut over the point) so much in vogue in certain Parisian *salles*, and then only against an adversary with an exceptionally low guard. She will probably do well, too, to eschew altogether, or to approach with the utmost diffidence, the use of the *Coup d'Arrêt* and the *Coup de temps*, or "time thrust,"—expedients as useful to a master as they are dangerous to a novice,—and she will doubtless with feminine instinct quickly appreciate the value of the elegant and insinuating *dérobé*.

How can I bring home to non-fencers or tyros the short sharp triumph of the *riposte*, the thrust delivered without lunging, which follows the successful parry of an attack, better than by saying it is an epigram or repartee in action, which, like its analogue, fails utterly if it be delivered a second too late? The "*Riposte du tac-au-tac*" is, perhaps, one of the supreme delights in life in the *salle d'armes* or out of it.

Later on, too, the fencer will have to decide for herself whether she will do fealty to the school of simple or of counter parries, or whether she will be warned in time, and, "giving unto Caesar the things that are Caesar's," will divide her favours equally. For the neophyte I can only here say that the *Contre*—like in number and designation to the *Simple*—is a circular parry; that is, a parry in which the point describes a circle in following the opponent's blade, bringing it back to the starting place.

The mention of classical and romantic schools just now awoke in me a desire to digress for a moment from the practical part of my subject to its historical aspect, and discuss briefly the relative claims of the two schools to superiority—claims as hotly disputed as by the literary partisans of the *Classiques et Romantiques* of 1830, or as the same burning question in regard to the English stage in the days of John Philip Kemble and of Edmund Kean. If I may take a histrionic illustration from our stage, I should call Danet the Garrick of the art of fence—forming the transition, the link between the cold and formal classicism of the Bettertons and Quins, *i.e.*, the Liancourts of the past, and the academic stateliness, the regularity and precision of Gomard, Cordelois, and Grisier, the Kembles of fencing; till we reach the *fougue*, brilliance, and lightning-like flashes of the great Bertrand—the Edmund Kean or Talma of the art, or, as his followers prefer to call him, the Napoleon of Fence: "*un tireur hors ligne parmi les tireurs hors ligne.*" "Taking a fencing lesson from Bertrand," says Legouvé, one of his pupils, "is like listening to Victor Hugo talking poetry, and Alexandre Dumas (father and son) talking drama."

Bazancourt, the author of the charming and impulsive "*Secrets de L'Epée*" (one of the few fencing books the amateur and non-fencer alike may read with pleasure), stands alone as an example of the purely Romantic, almost the "Fantastic," school. Let us call him the Frédéric Lemaître of the foil.

But I must drop these seductive comparisons, and come back to my practice.

One of the most important things in fencing, after accurate position on guard and precision in the lunge have been attained, is what is known as the *doigt*é, "fingering," or play of fingers, indispensable for the effectual accomplishment of feint or parry, the seat of it lying between the thumb and fore-finger. Such is the delicacy of movement requisite for the performance of the simplest operation in fencing, that not only must the shoulder be carefully kept out of play, but even the elbow and wrist must be held in a relatively passive state, the whole of the mental activity of the fencer being transferred to, and concentrated in, the fingers. "To think," says Legouvé, the *doyen* of French fencers, and one of the Immortals, "that such a complex act, in which the whole body takes part, is concentrated between the extremity of the thumb and first finger."

Then we have the changes of *Engagement*, the various methods of attack—the *Coup droit*, or straight lunge,—the *Dégagement*, or passing the blade under or over that of the opponent, and so changing the line,— the Counter-disengagement and the *Coupé* or "cut over the point," already alluded to. Of other feints, I must barely enumerate the *Pressure* (*Pression*), distinguishable from the *Beat* (*Battement*), the *Rub* or *Graze* (*Froissé*), and the *Binding* and envelopment of the blade (*Liement*),—each of which must be held for my present purpose to define itself, and all of which may be combined in endless variety with the various other attacks.

It is a platitude to say that a far better idea of all the various attacks and parries can be obtained in a few thorough lessons from a good master, foil in hand, than from hours of study given to books. Still, the teaching of the best masters may be reasoned out at leisure in the library; and I would especially draw attention to the advantage that may accrue to the student of fencing from the careful scrutiny and comparison of sets of good fencing plates. The value of a treatise on fencing may be almost said to depend entirely upon the quality of its illustrations; and if Angelo's great work may be called the "Libro d'Oro" of the art of fence, it is because his plates, drawn by Gwyn, and engraved by Chambers, Ryland, Hall, and Grignion——some of the best artists of the day——although often borrowed (notably by Diderot for his great *Encyclopédie*), and spoilt in the borrowing, have on the whole never been, and probably never will be, surpassed.

"The three words which compose the language of fencing," said Bazancourt, "are Judgment, Regularity, Rapidity"; and by "Judgment" he tells us he means, above all, "mistrust, ruse, foresight, the dumb interrogation of the sword, '*la justesse de l'appréciation par la pensée.*'" If for all this I may substitute the one word "tact," I think it becomes evident at once that women have only to take sword or foil in hand, and transpose the quality in which they socially most excel, to change the scene of its triumphant operation from the carpet of the drawing-room to the boards of the *salle d'armes*.

Again, listen to Legouvé's remarks upon the moral aspect of fencing, its reaction upon character:—

"It teaches you to judge men (and women). Dissimulation, foil in hand, is an impossibility. After a five minutes' assault the sham veneer of worldly hypocrisy drops off with the perspiration, like rouge, and in place of the man (or woman) of the world, kid-gloved, polite, with conventional phrase, you have before you the real man (or woman), thoughtful or frivolous, weak or strong, cunning or simple, sincere or false... The soul is never more distinctly shown than through the closely woven meshes of the wire mask."

I must send my readers desirous of more in the same strain to the fountain head, just as for a searching analysis of the physical effect of fencing upon the constitution of body and brain I must refer them to the closely-reasoned scientific exposition of M. Lagrange in his "Physiology of Bodily Exercise."

I have left myself but small space to pay a tribute to the few famous women who have been before their age in drawing sword or foil. Alas! that I can no longer claim for our sex the fencing triumphs achieved by the Chevalière d'Eon de Beaumont against Saint George, and the most famous swordsmen of his day; for modern criticism and, I believe, contemporary inquiry have both decided that the pretended *Chevalière* was really a *Chevalier*. But La Maupin (the original of Gautier's idealised heroine), who flourished (her blade) at the end of the seventeenth century, was undoubtedly a "fine dame," in the ordinary sense as well as in that of Rivarol's dictionary. How, insulted by Dumény the actor, she challenged him, and, on his declining her cartel, despoiled him of his watch and snuff-box; how she, in her turn, insulted a lady at a ball, and then "called out" and pinked to death one after another no fewer than three masculine champions of the said lady, returning to the ball, and subsequently obtaining the King's pardon, is a matter of history, or of *chronique scandaleuse*, and is perhaps better suited to point a moral than to be pointed at as an ensample.

For, indeed, fencing, of which I have tried, feebly enough, to depict the advantages and charms, does not owe any of these to its possible application to duelling purposes. Rather may it be said that modern fencing——fencing as a fine art, at any rate as a liberal art——has, in spite of what we see going on daily across the Channel, arisen phoenix-like from the ashes of duelling. And lest it should be thought that in speaking of fencing as a liberal art I have outstepped the bounds of "sweet reasonableness," let me, in conclusion, recall to my readers the words of a great writer lately gone from amongst us——whom no one will accuse of unduly pressing the claims of physical as against mental culture—and summon John Henry Newman to lend his eloquent voice to silence the seekers after utility:—

"There are bodily exercises which are liberal, and mental exercises which are not so... That alone is liberal which stands upon its own pretensions, which is independent of sequel, expects no complement, refuses to be informed by any end or absorbed into any art, in order duly to present itself to our contemplation...

"The most ordinary pursuits have this specific character if they are self-sufficient and complete; the highest lose it when they minister to something beyond them. It is absurd to balance in point of worth and importance a treatise on reducing fractions with a game of cricket or a fox-chase; yet of the two the bodily exercise has that quality which we call 'liberal,' and the intellectual has it not... Whenever present gain is the motive, still more distinctive effect has it upon the character of a given pursuit; thus racing, which was a liberal exercise in Greece, forfeits its value in times like these, so far as it is made the occasion of gambling.

"All that I have been now saying is summed up in a few characteristic words of the great philosopher:— 'Of possessions,' he says, 'those rather are useful which bear fruit; those liberal which tend to enjoyment. By fruitful, I mean which yield revenue; by enjoyable, where nothing accrues of consequence beyond the using.'"

Is it not time that women should have a larger part in this "liberal art" of fencing, and so get within their grasp one instrument more, making for the physical, mental, and moral culture and perfection of themselves and of their children?

PUSHKIN PRESS—THE LONDON LIBRARY

"FOUND ON THE SHELVES"

THE LONDON LIBRARY (a registered charity) is one of the
UK's leading literary institutions and a favourite haunt of
authors, researchers and keen readers.

Membership is open to all.

Join at www.londonlibrary.co.uk.

www.pushkinpress.com